BREAKTHROUGHS

BROKEN OUT/THROUGH (2 SAMUEL 5:20)

BAAL PERAZIM!

CHELSEA KONG

PRINTED IN 2024, MADE IN TORONTO, CANADA
ISBN 978-1-990399-61-9
LIBRARY AND ARCHIVES CANADA

WHAT IS IT?

WHAT ARE BREAKTHROUGHS?

JOB

HEALTH

IT CAN BE ANYTHING
YOU NEED.

THE DEVIL LOVES TO TRAP, TRICK, AND LIE TO US.

DON'T LET THE DEVIL WIN!

PRAY UNTIL SOMETHING HAPPENS. (EPHESIANS 6:18)

KEEP YOUR EYES ON THE GOAL! (PHILIPPIANS 3:14)

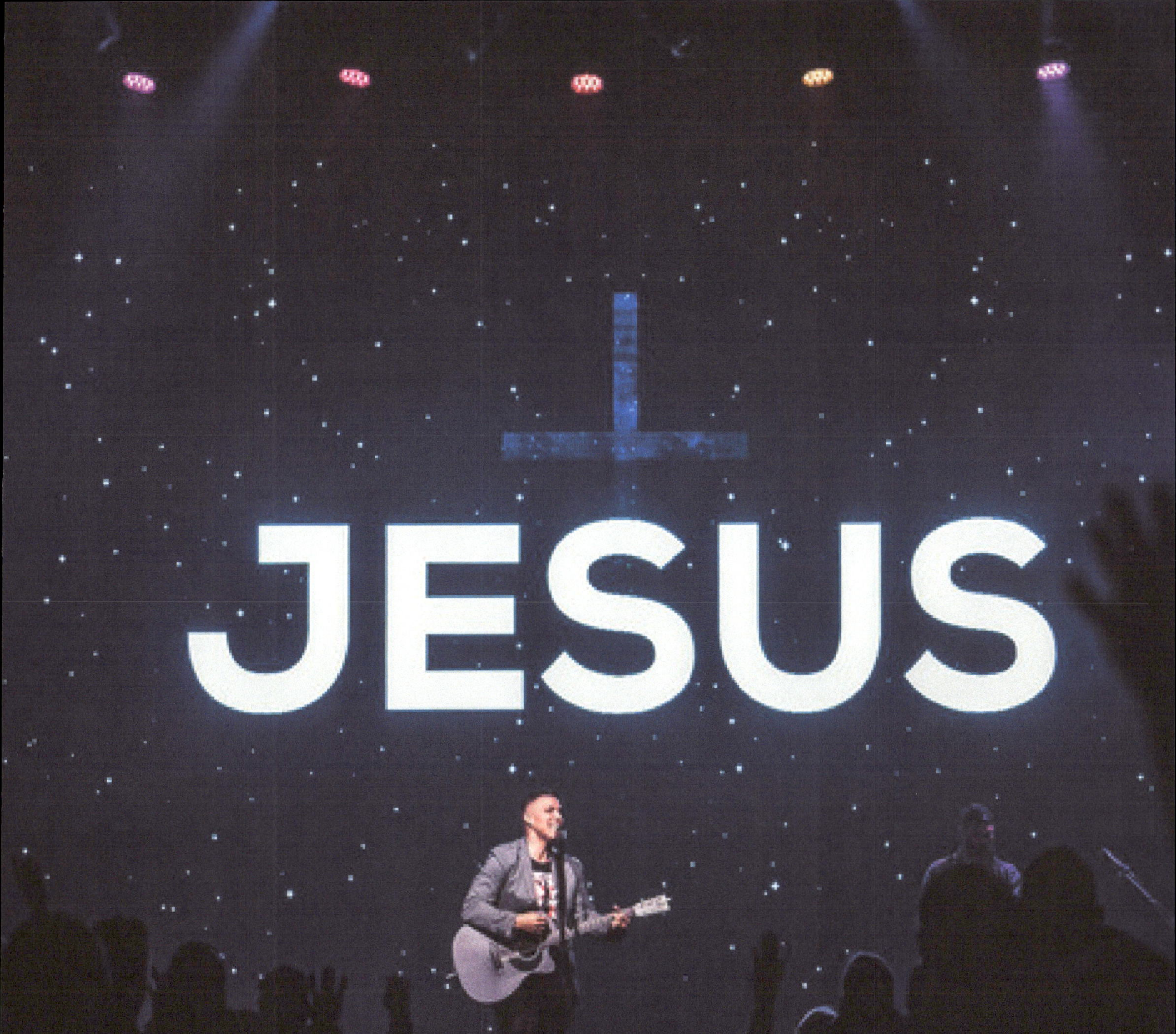
JESUS

KEEP SPEAKING GOD'S WORD.

WE MUST FIGHT BY THE
SPIRIT OF GOD.
(EPHESIANS 6:10)

WE LIVE BY GOD'S WORD.
(MATTHEW 4:4)

PLEAD THE BLOOD OF JESUS.

GOD'S WORD IS A SWORD.(ACTS 1:8)

ASK OTHERS TO PRAY FOR YOU.

KEEP GOING TO CHURCH.

HOLY COMMUNION HELPS
IF YOU ARE BAPTIZED.

STOP

STOP THE DEVIL WITH GOD'S WORD.

FIGHT THE DEVIL
WITH GOD'S WORD.

GUARD YOUR HEART FROM THE DEVIL'S WORDS.

USE GOD'S WORD
AGAINST THE DEVIL.

PSALM 91

TRAMPLE THE DEVIL UNDER YOUR FEET.

FAITH OVER FEAR

HAVE FAITH IN GOD'S WORD
THAT YOU HAVE IT.

HOLY SPIRIT GIVES US POWER.(ACTS 1:8)

ASK THE LORD TO GIVE YOU A VISION.

STAY IN GOD'S PRESENCE.
(PSALM 16:11)

STAY STRONG IN THE LORD!
FIGHT WELL (1 TIMOTHY 6:12)

SPEAK OUT WHAT YOU SEE IN THE VISION.

GIVE THANKS THAT
YOU HAVE IT!

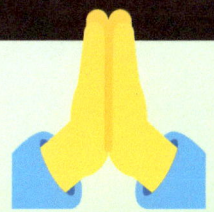

WORSHIP AND PRAISE
UNTIL SOMETHING HAPPENS.

TIME TO Celebrate

CELEBRATE YOUR VICTORY!

CELEBRATE WITH OTHERS.

HAPPY BIRTHDAY

BIRTHDAYS OPEN DOORS
FOR GOD TO BLESS YOU!

ASK GOD EVERY BIRTHDAY FOR BREAKTHROUGHS.

SHARE GOD'S GOODNESS.

SALVATION PRAYER

God, I know I sinned against you. Forgive me for the wrong that I have done. I believe that Jesus Christ died on the cross for me. That He rose from the grave so that after three days. I can have His long-lasting life. Come into my heart to be my Lord and Savior. I choose to turn away from my sins and I choose to follow you. Lead me to walk with you. Keep me safe and teach me your ways. Stop every bad thing in my life that has an open door to hurt me. Close those doors. Holy Spirit fill me now in Jesus' name. Amen.

BAPTISM IN THE HOLY SPIRIT

Jesus, you are the one that fills me with Your Spirit. Come Holy Spirit and come into my life and fill me to overflow with Your presence. Come with your fire too. Thank you for the gift of tongues in Jesus' name. Amen.

Open your mouth and let the words come out that God gives you. It will be words that you don't know what they mean. You can ask God what it means. You need to let Him talk through you every day to grow this gift.

He will bring you closer to God and you will know Jesus more. You will have power from God to do great things and know things.

PRAYER

Father God, thank you for the power of prayer. Thank you for breakthroughs! I pray to stop all the devil's plans against me. I pray for your plans to come now in Jesus' name. God rebuke Satan for stealing from me and that he must pay 7 times back to me and my family in Jesus' name. Thank you for everything that is mine to come to me. Teach me how to use them well for you, Jesus. Keep my heart in your ways and to do your plan in Jesus' name. Holy Spirit, help me know how to pray and what to do every day in Jesus' name. Amen.

2 CORINTHIANS 10:4

Message from the Author

Breakthroughs are God's way to work for us when the devil stops us from having God's best. He hates those who belong to God. He doesn't want us to have things from God. Jesus has all the power and authority and He gave it to us too. We can, stop the devil from stealing from us. We can ask God to make the devil give us back everything he stole and 7x more. We can through prayer and speaking, God's Word, command Satan to give us everything that he stole from our family too. We can stop all his plans pray God's plans to be done. God will bring us to have them. We can make him give us back our time and money, too.

OTHER PRODUCTS

Knowing God

How to Hear God's Voice

New Life in Jesus

Loving Israel

God's Gifts/Spiritual Talents

Meeting God

Word Power

Fruit of the Spirit

The Tabernacle

Bride for Jesus

A Life of Prayer

Live Free

Who am I in Jesus

Walk in Love

God's Favor

Man of God

Woman of God

How to Use Money

God's Wisdom

Fasting

See Jerusalem and Bethany

First Fruit Offering

Feast of Trumpets

Day of Atonement

Feast of Tabernacles

Counting the Omer

Festival of Lights

Glory, Presence, and Holy Spirit

Live in God's Presence

Pentecost

See Galilee, Nazareth, and Tiberias

Hear God Speak

Knowing Jesus

Knowing Holy Spirit

A Healthy Life and Healthy Life Work Book

Smokey the Cat

Passover Unleavened Bread

Resurrection Life

The Blessing

Revival

Chelsea Learns Hebrew

Give Thanks

Thanksgiving

Jesus' Birth

Proverbs 31 Woman

OTHER PRODUCTS

Loving Jesus: Bride and Groom

Colours in the Bible

Coming soon

An Eagle's Life

Open Doors

ABC's of Faith

Puzzle Books

Biblical Puzzle Book Vol 1-5

Bible Puzzles for Young Children Book 1-3

Biblical Puzzle for Children Books 1-5

Devotionals

31 Day Devotional

Inspirational/Other

Chelsea's Psalms and Poems

Your Daily Meal: Chelsea's Food

Teaching Series

How to Hear God's Voice Teaching Guide & Audio Book

Relationship with God, Jesus, Holy Spirit Guide

Knowing God, Jesus, Holy Spirit Guide & Audio Book

Flowing in the Prophetic

Teaching (Non-Sale on my website)

Purim

Passover

Resurrection

More books to come!

BOOK REVIEWS

More books on Amazon, Kobo, and Barnes and Noble, Smashwords, and IngramSpark.
https://chelseak532002550.wordpress.com/

More books on Amazon, Kobo, and Barnes and Noble, Smashwords, and IngramSpark.
https://www.amazon.com/author/chelseakong

Please leave a review and share with friends to help the author continue to write more books to reach more readers. Thank you so much for your support.

Review!

About
CHELSEA KONG

She is a writer, creative arts and digital media artist, skilled administration and payroll professional, and podcaster. Chelsea also served in a variety of roles, from audiovisual, photography, to assisting on the worship team, and ministry team. She also has a passion for families being united.

Chelsea has been a guest on Unity Live Radio, The Lady Tracey Show, and How to Live for Christ and is highly recommended by a Proud Christian blog. She is also a guest blogger. A few of her books have been featured in YourAuthorHub, etc. She graduated from Hotel and Restaurant Management, Digital Media Arts, Office Administration, Payroll Professional, and experience working with children. Chelsea lives in Toronto, Canada. She mainly writes children's books, stories, bridal writing, poems, lyrics for songs, words of encouragement, blessings, prayers, and jokes. The author of How to Hear the Voice of God, the Bridal Collection, Knowing God, etc. She also has her own Bible Puzzle books and other inspired products. Her podcast channel is called Chelsea K on Anchor, Spotify, and iTunes.

Please check my website to find out more:
https://chelseak532002550.wordpress.com/

www.ingramcontent.com/pod-product-compliance
Lightning Source LLC
LaVergne TN
LVHW072134070426
835513LV00003B/103